Offline
101^Activities
You Can Do With Your Child

Offline
101 ^Activities
You Can Do With Your Child

By Steve and Ruth Bennett

****

BPT Press
P.O. Box 834
Randolph, MA 02368-0834

101 Offline Activities You Can Do With Your Child
Copyright © 2011 by Steve and Ruth Bennett

For information, address BPT Press, P.O. Box 834, Randolph, MA 02368-0834 or email info@bptpress.com.

Book cover design by Jessica Marony and Deborah Beaudoin
Page composition by Peter Martin

ACKNOWLEDGEMENTS

Many thanks to friends and family members who contributed great ideas and helped test the activities in this book to make sure that they're easy to do and, most importantly, have a high GB (giggle bytes) factor. Special thanks go to Stacey Miller for her work not only on the original books, but on conceptualizing a new, streamlined volume and shepherding it through production. Thanks to Kristine Hansen and Peter Martin for their wonderful production work. Finally, a swish of the tail goes to Messrs. Smoots and Smittens for not taking a five claw discount on our stash of yarn, string, and other goodies that we use to develop crafts activities and simple games. Your restraint is amazing – you ARE truly noble beasts.

CONTENTS

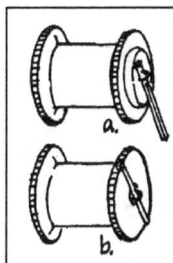

13. Clothing Designer

14. Coffee Filter Painting

15. Common Threads

16. Crazy Street Signs

17. Creature Dinner Party

18. Drawing Derby

19. Easy Abacus

20. Flash in the Pan

21. Folding Screen

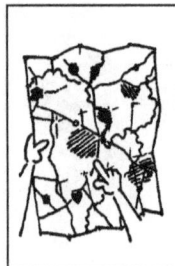

22. Follow Me

23. Foodcaster

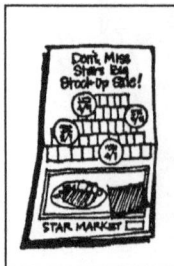

24. Fresh Off the Press

25. Gimme Shelter

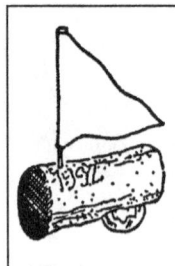

26. Go Boating

27. Godzilla Returns (Again)

28. Great Wiper Ensemble

29. Guess That Sound

30. Hat Potato

31. Hat Trimming

32. Heads Up

33. Hotel Counts

34. How Long Before…?

35. Humdinger

36. Indoor Treasure Hunts

37. In-Flight Map Game Pack

38. Invisible Kids

39. It's Great to Be…

40. Kitchen Bowling and Other Sports

41. Label Master

42. Log Those Plates!

43. Macaroni Math

44. Magical Mystery Machine

45. Make an Ad

46. Make-Before-You-Go Card Game Board

47. Make-Before-You-Go Mileage Bags

48. Make-Before-You-Go Swiss Army Notebook

49. Make-Believe on the Range

50. Modern Conveniences

51. More Than Meets the Eye

52. Muffin Tin Toss

53. Museum Scavenger Hunt

54. My Strangest Case

55. Mystery Story

56. Navigator's Hat

57. No "Ors," "Ands," (or) "Buts"

58. Noah's Noodle Maze

59. Noah's Noodle Stamps and Brushes

60. Number Hunt

61. Off-the-Cuff

62. Oversized Homemade Checkers

63. Pass the Exits

64. Patterns

65. People Food

66. Pin the Food on the Plate

67. Ping-Pong Potpourri

68. Repealing Newton's Law

69. Rosetta Stones

70. Scrambled Recipes

71. Sensational Salon

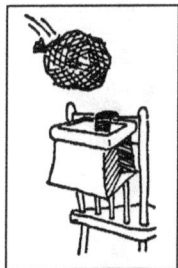
72. Shooting Hoops

73. Sign Jumbles

74. Sink or Swim

75. Smiling Violations

76. Snork!

77. Soundalikes

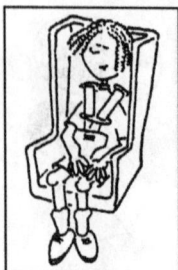

78. Sounds Like…

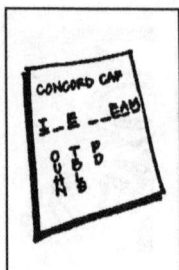

79. Speedy Word-Guessers

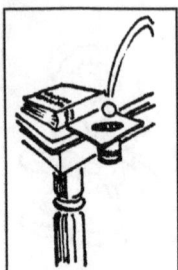

80. Tabletop Basketball

81. Time Travelers

82. Trailblazers

83. Trained Guesses

84. Travel Tally

85. Traveling Board Games

86. You (and Me) Tube Heads

87. Tunnel Vision

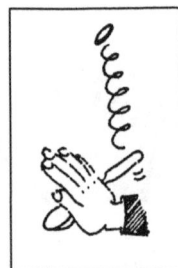

88. Two-Bit Tiddlywinks

89. Upside Down

90. Vegetable Art

91. Waitperson of the Hour

92. Wall Mural

93. What Character!

94. What Did You Say!

95. What Would They Do?

96. Which Thing Came First?

97. Who Knows What Fun Lurks...

98. Witches' Brew

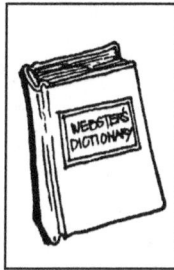
99. With Apologies to Mr. Webster

100. Word Family Game

101. Word Games Galore

INTRODUCTION

Much has changed since we wrote our first activity book for parents and caregivers, *365 TV-Free Activities You Can Do With Your Child*. At that time, television was the primary competitor for human interaction in a household. Computers were a luxury and the only electronic gadgets you could carry in your pocket were the TV remote or garage door opener.

Today, of course, television is but one of many electronic devices that vie for our attention from the moment we wake up to the moment we sink into sleep. Smart phones. Game consoles. eBook Readers. Laptops. Netbooks. Internet tablets. In-car video systems. In-pocket audio systems. If you're awake, you're plugged in, literally or via wireless waves.

Now, this isn't a Luddite rant. In fact, we love this digital stuff. It's incredibly fun, useful, and convenient (who knows—you might be reading this text on an e-reader or tablet of some sort). It allows us to work and exercise our creativity in ways not possible just a few years ago. And it enables us to cut through time and space and connect with people who otherwise would be out of sight, out of mind.

But . . . there's still something fundamentally satisfying about relying solely on the electronic activity in our brains and muscles to entertain ourselves and connect with family members and friends. Whether it's a simple guessing game or a more elaborate round of toilet-paper tube bowling, low-tech/no-tech games and activities are remarkably satisfying, rejuvenating, and, most importantly, a great way to engage your children.

Will kids actually want to do non-electronic "offline" activities and games? You bet. Because as corny as it might sound, your children still want something that doesn't come in a box, doesn't require a battery or AC cord, and doesn't require firmware updates: you. Yep, you, the superhero who can leap tall buildings and keep the universe on track. And that doesn't mean "you, 24/7"—short activity sessions throughout the day is all it takes. Try a round of "Soundalikes" while you're standing in line at the supermarket or waiting for your appointment at the doctor's office. Postpone Internet surfing for 30 minutes for a round of blindfold games (the Web sites you were going to view will still be there when you're done. One of the great things about the Net is that you can use it on *your* schedule). Try "Muffin Tin Toss" while you're making dinner instead of using the TV, game console, or computer as a way to buy some cooking time.

In the following pages, you're bound to find offline activities that strike a chord. Many involve little or no preparation, and when materials are needed, you're likely to have them in your recycle bin (sorry, no extended warranties on toilet paper kazoos—when the kazoo crashes, get another tube).

We've found, and have been told by readers, that the most satisfying approach is to let your kids pick out activities that they'd like to do (pre-readers can make choices based on the visual table of contents). Encourage your children to come up with their own variations. Flip your own creativity switch and come with alternatives yourself. Other than obvious rules related to safety, the only rule is this: have fun!

Steve and Ruth Bennett

Cambridge, Massachusetts

May 2011

Adventure Treks

1

Intrepid explorers have to know how to avoid dangers like boiling-hot lava flows, alligators, snakes, crevices, and quicksand. Choose your peril; your floor is now covered with it!

To escape the danger, your young adventurers need to place stepping stones across the hazards. The stepping stones can include towels, throw pillows, sheets of paper, old clothes, and sofa cushions. As the kids try to get around the house without touching the floor, they can extend their path by adding more stepping stones in strategic locations. They can also incorporate beds, chairs, and sofas as "solid ground."

Encourage your children to create an adventure story to go along with the game. Perhaps they're space explorers on a distant volcanic planet or naturalists in the alligator-infested swamps of the Everglades. Either way, they'd better try to make it safely back to their space-swamp vehicle (you might recognize it as a couch).

Whatever you do, don't fall in. . . .

REQUIRED
- towels
- sheets of paper
- throw pillows
- couch cushions
- old clothes

CATEGORY
At Home

2

Alphabet Game

REQUIRED
• your time only

Here's a simple word game that puts a new twist on making an alphabetical list of items. The longer the game goes on, the more there is to remember, and the harder it gets. Play it while traveling, doing errands around town, or at home.

One player starts by saying a word that starts with "A". You and your children can decide beforehand if you want to limit the choice of words to a particular category (things that move, buildings, things in the environment, etc.). The next player repeats the "A" word, then adds one that starts with "B." The third repeats the growing list, then adds a word starting with "C," and so on. For example, the first player may say "automobile." Player two might say "automobile, bus." Player three might say "automobile, bus, car," and so on, until the list gets too long to remember.

You can allow players to skip difficult letters like "Q", "X", and "Z". And for a variation, have your kids try to do the alphabet backwards.

So how about a category of things we'd like to do on our first visit to the moon?

CATEGORY
Anytime, Anyplace

Archie's Tractor

3

⚠ **adult supervision**

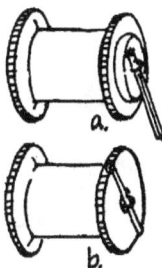

Here's an ingenious little mobile toy that Ruth's dad enjoyed during his childhood. It's strong enough to climb up a book, but it's not motorized.

First find a wooden spool and a small, thin bar of soap. Shape a sliver of soap so that it is about the size and shape of a Lifesaver candy (your job). Remove the flammable end of a kitchen match (your job, again). Place the piece of soap on one end of the spool and thread a small rubber band through the hole in the soap and spool. Insert the matchstick through the end of the rubber band next to the soap to keep it from pulling through (see "a").

On the other end of the spool, cut a long recess (your job) so that when a piece of toothpick (slightly less than the diameter of the spool) is laid across the hole and is inserted through the other end of the stretched rubber band, it won't rotate (see "b"). Fine-tune your machine by experimenting with different kinds of rubber bands.

Adjust the matchstick so that part of it protrudes an inch beyond the edge of the spool. Use this end as a crank to wind the rubber band until it's taut, then place the "tractor" on the table and let it rip!

REQUIRED
- **wooden thread spool**
- **matchstick**
- **toothpick**
- **rubber band**
- **soap**

CATEGORY
At Home

4 Audrey's Tic-Tac-Toe Game

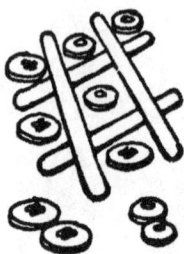

REQUIRED

- popsicle sticks or chopsticks
- vegetables
- placemat or plate

What's the most exciting way to play tic-tac-toe? According to our daughter, Audrey, it's: Winner eats all!

Your kids can play this game of edible tic-tac-toe on a placemat or plate with clean Popsicle sticks or chopsticks. (You can play, too, while you cook; it's a great way to have fun while something is simmering or baking.) The sticks are used to form the traditional tic-tac-toe grid. For playing pieces, slice two different vegetables, say carrots and cucumbers (cut enough to play three or four games). The carrots represent the Xs, and the cucumbers the Os, or vice versa. Of course, both children can eat the pieces after a game; perhaps the winner gets to choose different vegetables that will be used as playing pieces for the next round.

Not only will your kids improve their tic-tac-toe technique and pass some enjoyable time while you're working on dinner, but they'll get a healthy snack in the process!

CATEGORY
In the Kitchen

Audrey's Tic-Tac-Tongs

If you've saved a few playing pieces from Audrey's Tic-Tac-Toe game and are looking for a greater challenge, try this variation.

Make the tic-tac-toe grid as before with Popsicle sticks or chopsticks on a clean placemat or plate, and give each child some vegetable playing pieces—carrots, celery, broccoli, representing Os and Xs. Now for the challenge: instead of using their fingers, the players use tongs (barbecue or salad) to move the pieces. Older kids can use chopsticks.

Play as usual, with the added twist that if a player drops a piece before moving it to the desired square, the other player gets an extra turn. Or for a really zany game, if a piece drops before reaching its target, place it in the square closest to where it lands and remove whatever piece was there. This can work either for or against the player. Hotshot players can take the ultimate tic-tac-tong test: moving pieces with their eyes closed!

Ready, set, grab those tongs!

REQUIRED
- popsicle sticks or chopsticks
- vegetables
- tongs
- placemat or plate

CATEGORY
In the Kitchen

6

Big-Time Newspaper

Extra, extra! Read all about it! Kids launch new media venture while parents cook supper! Dinner finished in record time!

Your kids can make their own headlines on a giant newspaper "printed" on your kitchen table. After covering the table with large sheets of paper or opened paper bags taped together, your junior reporters can begin writing about zany "news" events.

To get the general look of a newspaper, your kids should write their newspaper's name in large letters, as well as some headlines and columns. The stories can be about anything, but suggest that your kids start with fanciful food stories to tie into the dinner spirit. The lead article might be: "Giant Meatball from Mars Lands on Shadybrook Elementary School! Principal Says: 'We'll Cover It in Noodles!'" After writing the headlines in large letters, your kids can draw some pictures to illustrate the articles.

Dinnertime will become chuckle time as the family reads stories aloud; encourage everybody to pick up where the articles left off and continue the story lines.

OK, stop the presses . . . and pass the ketchup!

REQUIRED
- paper or bags for covering table
- art supplies
- tape

CATEGORY
In the Kitchen

Bistro Spy

The old "I Spy" game can be a sanity saver when your kids are ready to eat but the restaurant is on its own schedule. Here are a few variations that can turn waiting time into instant fun time.

If you're waiting for a table to be cleared, start off a "spy" session by selecting various objects in the entry area, such as the coat rack, the maitre d's microphone, the cash register, plants, and various decorations for your kids to guess. Get creative with older kids by offering clues that are more cryptic than the standard "I spy something purple". For instance, you might say, "I spy something with a mouth that occasionally opens and swallows flat, rectangular green objects and round, shiny disks" (the cash register).

Once you're seated, select objects around the table, such as art on the menu, placemats, napkins, advertising placards, art on the walls, and so on. Don't forget subtle items such as wallpaper, designs in the carpet, and silverware patterns.

Won't everyone be happy when you can call out, "I spy something coming from the kitchen and headed our way?"

REQUIRED
• your time only

CATEGORY
Out and About

8

⚠ adult supervision

Blindfold Games

As kids, most of us played pin the tail on the donkey at birthday parties. But that's just one of many blindfold games that your child can do to pass the time during cabin-bound days (see next activity for more ideas).

Blindfold toss, for example, will challenge even the most athletically-minded child. Place three or four pots or bowls on the floor and assign point values to each one. Blindfold your child and have him or her toss several rolled-up pairs of socks at the target containers. Then try it yourself. Perhaps the object is to get the most or least points (perhaps assign negative or "penalty" points to some containers) or to get all the socks in a bin of a certain color. It's harder than it sounds!

Once the tossing games are over, have your child keep the blindfold on, then try putting on a hat, coat, or glove (or tying his or her shoes). You try it, too.

Finally, older kids (and perhaps you) will enjoy trying to make change while wearing the blindfold. Oops, did you really mean to give away $1.50 in change for that $1 bill?

REQUIRED
- blindfold
- socks
- pots or bowls
- hats
- coats
- gloves
- coins

CATEGORY
At Home

Blindfold Games Revisited

If your child enjoyed the games in the previous activity, these are sure to be a hit.

Put the blindfold on your child and break out the paper, crayons, and markers. Then let your child choose something to draw: perhaps a person, a landscape, an animal, or an object. As your child is creating the masterpiece, ask what part of the drawing he or she is working on and what colors he or she is using. You're bound to hear some amusing answers.

A variation of this activity is to call out shapes for your child to draw: For instance, draw a box inside a box inside a box or five interlocking circles. You can also call out elements of a picture: Draw a man balancing on a ball and holding his left arm in the air. Add a tree next to the man. Place a bird in the tree, and a cloud. A cloud in the sky. Who knows where the bird will wind up!

Finally, try this one on your child: Have him or her draw a clock with the hands at, say, eight o'clock. Be realistic, though; if that happens to be bedtime, your child might have difficulty drawing it even without a blindfold.

REQUIRED
- blindfold
- art supplies

CATEGORY
At Home

10

Careers

REQUIRED
• writing supplies
• bowl, paper bag or hat

What does your child want to be when he or she grows up? Here's how you can find out.

On slips of paper, write down various job titles (use your own, your spouse's, or a friend's for inspiration). Make sure you include a variety of jobs (and feel free to include such zany positions as dinosaur trainer, bungee jumper, and haystack builder). Fold the papers in half and put them into a bowl, paper bag, or hat. Pick a job title from the hat, then act out "a day at the workplace" and see if your child can guess which job you're portraying.

Encourage your child to ask questions that will help uncover the job title: "Do you work indoors or outdoors?" "Do you work alone or with others?" "Is any special equipment required to do your job?" Then reverse roles and see if you can figure out the job title your child has chosen.

So, did you find any interesting possibilities for a second career?

CATEGORY
At Home

Categories Unlimited

11

The best thing about word games is that you can play along with your kids and still keep an eye on your cooking. Here's one that's sure to help your kids pass the time before supper.

Your child names a category such as a color, then you, and he or she, take turns naming representative foods. The color red, for example, might bring to mind "apple," "pomegranate," "rhubarb," and "radish." When all the colors are exhausted, you can use other categories, such as "sweet foods" or "foods that can be eaten only with a spoon."

REQUIRED
• your time only

You can also use non-food categories, such as kitchen gadgets, appliances, or other cooking-related items.

See who can come up with the most items in a category, the most unusual item, or even the most unusual category. To make the game even more exciting, try naming the items in the category in alphabetical order!

CATEGORY
At Home

12 Changing Rooms

REQUIRED
• your time only

Here's an activity that will turn any room of your home into an amusement park for the mind. And you won't have to turn it upside down either!

The idea is to have your child focus on a room in your home or some part of the room and then close his or her eyes. You then alter something and see if he or she can figure out what's different. For example, let's say that your living room has a stack of magazines on a coffee table, and the top magazine happens to have a red cover. Then, while his or her eyes are closed, you can place a different magazine on top.

You can also rearrange hats on a hatrack, place an area rug upside down, or conduct other little bits of chicanery that won't cause anyone extra work to tidy up (you might suggest a rule that the room changer puts everything back the way it was after a round of guessing has taken place).

Say, do you suppose there's always been a mitten hanging on that ficus tree by the window?

CATEGORY
At Home

Clothing Designer

You've probably never thought of your kitchen as Savile Row. Well, here's an activity tailor-made to keep your child busy creating while you're busy cooking.

On a table covered with a large sheet of paper, your child can draw life-size clothes—fit for a life-size paper doll.

First, he or she can lie on the paper (put it on the floor first) while you quickly trace his or her body. Once the outline is back on the table, your child can fill in the clothes. The attire can be as fanciful or as fancy as your child's imagination allows. What about a knight in shining silver armor? A princess at the royal ball? Or even a mermaid or a centaur?

Another alternative is to take a jacket, pair of pants, or some other article of clothing, lay it on the paper, and trace around it. Then your child can color in the clothes and cut them out. Or he or she can draw in a head, hands, feet, and other features to make a colorful paper person.

Of course, your designer can tape the clothing to him- or herself. Voila! A walking, talking paper doll!

REQUIRED

- paper or bags for covering table

- art supplies

CATEGORY
At Home

14

Coffee Filter Painting

A hot cup of coffee is often the best way to get the grown-ups going in the kitchen. With this fun painting idea, coffee filters will get your children going—and keep them entertained.

Because of their absorbency, coffee filters make an unusual painting surface for water colors—a single touch of the brush to the filter will produce a splash of color. Just set up your children with a few coffee filters and some water colors and watch their creativity perk up. Your kids can also use water with food coloring instead of paints. (Either way, put newspapers on the table or floor before the painting begins.)

You might also suggest that, while you're cooking, your children cut coffee filters into interesting shapes or glue two or more together. A flat-bottomed filter, for example, can be cut down along the side folds and opened to make a great butterfly. Your kids can also tape their creations to the kitchen window to create a stained-glass effect.

When your children brew up this kind of fun, time in the kitchen won't just seem like the same old grind!

REQUIRED
- coffee filters
- water color paints or food coloring
- brushes
- newspapers

CATEGORY
In the Kitchen

Common Threads

15

If your kids enjoy guessing games, then this activity will probably be a hit with them. The object of the game is to have one person list items that fit an unnamed category and have everyone else try to figure out what the category is.

Let's say that the child giving the clues is thinking of the category "things with wheels." He or she might list "bicycle," "roller skates," "cars," "trucks," "airplanes," and "shopping carts." After each clue is given, everyone gets a chance to guess the category, and the first one to get the right answer goes on to give the next set of clues.

As a variation for older children, you can have players limit their clues to things they see around them that fit the secret category.

OK, what category do these fall under? "Look out the window," "eat at restaurants," "visit museums," "collect seashells," "take day hikes," "play games," and "stay in hotels or motels." Give up? It's "things we like to do on vacation!"

REQUIRED
• your time only

CATEGORY
Anytime, Anyplace

16 Crazy Street Signs

REQUIRED
• your time only

Stuck in traffic? Pass some time by turning work and road signs into wacky, funny messages.

To make the game challenging for all, suggest a couple of simple ground rules (after that, anything goes!). First, a player can only change one word on the sign. Second, the word that gets changed must begin with the same letter as the word that takes its place. As an alternative, you might try substituting words that rhyme for the words in the sign.

Take the "Men at Work" sign over that manhole. That sign could become "Martians at Work." Or that "No Trespassing" sign can become "No Trampolining" or "No Trapeze Acts." And that bothersome "No Parking Zone?" Why not make it the "No Barking Zone!"

Excuse me, Bowser—can't you read the sign?

CATEGORY
Out and About

Creature Dinner Party

What if your pet goldfish threw a party and everybody—all the other animals, that is—came?

As you prepare dinner, imagine with your child that one of your family pets, or another animal, is having a dinner party, and the two of you have been asked to plan the gala affair.

First, have your child make up a guest list. Perhaps Highway, the guppy, would like to ask Fish One, the goldfish, and the rest of the fish in your tank to the bash. And, for variety, Highway also wants to include non-fish creatures such as Charlotte and Emily (a couple of felines) and Hobbes and Meendrah (a hamster duo). Of course, other guests can include zoo and farm animals.

Then have your child create a menu with foods sure to be enjoyed by all the guests. Encourage your child to include a variety so that there's something for everybody, such as fish flakes, cat chow, and hamster nibbles.

Your child can also list decorations that would be appropriate for the party. Perhaps coral reefs would make the fish and the sea animals feel right at home!

REQUIRED
• writing materials

CATEGORY
In the Kitchen

18

Drawing Derby

Here's how you can turn simple drawings into a fun group activity and a good Rx for the "cabin fever blues."

Set up a table with a sheet of paper and a chair for each child and have plenty of markers or crayons on hand. Next, have your kids suggest enough drawing topics so that there's one for everybody. Label each sheet of drawing paper with a separate topic. (As an alternative to separate sheets, you can cover the entire table with one large sheet of paper.)

REQUIRED
• drawing
  supplies

Once all the kids are ready with a blank sheet and a drawing topic, have them start drawing. After a short time (about one minute) have everyone stop drawing, move one seat to the right, and continue with the picture at that seat. Keep going until all the kids have contributed something to each drawing.

For a variation, you can give each child one or two markers so that they all have different colors, and have them keep their markers with them as they move. That way, they can look back at all the pictures and identify which part they added.

CATEGORY
At Home

On your mark, get set, draw!

Easy Abacus

19

Is your child a budding mathematical genius? Then why not help him or her make a ziti abacus?

Use a shoebox as the frame. Punch eight holes in the box, four in each end, spaced evenly. Thread a string through the first bottom hole and knot it so that it can't slip out. Then thread nine pieces of ziti through the string. Slip the string through the first top hole. Now weave the string through the remaining top and bottom holes, adding nine pieces of ziti to each strand.

The first strand, starting from the right, represents the "ones" column; the second strand, the "tens"; the third, the "hundreds"; and the fourth strand represents the "thousands" column. Each piece of ziti represents one digit, so that two pieces of ziti in the second column equals "20," three pieces in the third column is "300," and so forth. Your child can use the abacus to do some low-tech mathematical computations by raising and lowering pieces of ziti and "reading" the results.

So, what's a plateful of ziti plus a ladleful of spaghetti sauce?

REQUIRED
- shoebox
- uncooked ziti
- string

CATEGORY
At Home

20

Flash in the Pan

Rustling up some dinner in this hectic world makes the microwave a great helper. Here's a way for your kids to build their own play appliance.

A small carton, like a shoebox, works great as a microwave. All your child has to do to start is set the shoebox on its side. If he or she wants the door to swing open, just tape one end of the lid to the box. On the front of the lid, paste a piece of white paper, then have your child draw a window so everyone can "see" the food cooking inside the oven.

REQUIRED
- shoebox
- small round plastic lid
- tape or glue
- art supplies

Next to the window, draw a time display, a touch pad, or any dials or switches your child wants. A small round plastic lid inside the box becomes a carousel. Your child can even personalize the microwave with a nameplate.

To serve up a tasty dinner, kids can place some pretend food or some real gourmet fare (crackers or cereal) in a small bowl, put it in the microwave, and "zap" it for a minute or two. How about that—dinner in seconds, and no chance of overcooking the food!

CATEGORY
At Home

Folding Screen

This folding screen is something your kids will have fun making and using for a long time.

To make the basic screen, use three or four large pieces of heavy cardboard; the sides from an appliance box work very well. If the box is intact, cut open one corner so that the sides are still connected and fold it accordion-style so that it stands up. If your children are starting with separate pieces of cardboard, make connecting hinges with strips of duct tape.

Now you can have your children decorate their folding screen using paints, markers, and pictures clipped from magazines (depending on the type of decorations they chose to apply, your children may want to first cover the cardboard with sheets of paper more suitable for coloring).

When the screen is done, your children can use it to enclose a reading nook or perhaps to designate where the playroom ends and the shores of a getaway tropical island begin.

REQUIRED
- cardboard
- duct tape (if cardboard is separate sheets)
- art supplies
- magazines and other picture sources

CATEGORY
At Home

22

Follow Me

REQUIRED
• two copies of
  the same map

This map game for kids with reading and arithmetic skills will reveal the best route from A to B and is a great way to avoid backseat boredom.

To do this activity, you'll need two copies of the same map, preferably for the area you are driving through. Make sure the maps indicate the miles between cities or towns, or between exits. Give one map to your child and keep one for yourself. Start at an easy-to-find location (point it out to your child), and give travel directions based on the roads, landmarks, intersections, and mileage shown on the map (you might have to point out the mileage numbers on the various road segments).

For example, you might say, "Take 1-80 west for fifteen miles; take Route 4 north to the next town; and take Route 11 toward the lake for seven miles." Then ask your child where he or she is on the map, and see if you have both "arrived" at the same location!

As a variation, have your child pick the route for you to follow. You can point out a destination on the map and have your child give directions to get there.

CATEGORY
On the Road

Just follow the directions to fun ahead!

Foodcaster

Sports stars get play-by-play coverage when they perform—why not Mom and Dad when they're working in the kitchen?

All you need is a large spoon to turn your kitchen into a broadcast booth. Hand the spoon over to your kids, and suggest that they tell the "audience" what's going on in the kitchen. Sometimes it helps to give them a quick twenty-second demonstration—just hold the spoon in front of your face like an old-time microphone and start off your performance patter.

REQUIRED
• large spoon

"It's a beautiful day here in Smith Kitchen Stadium," you might say if you want to give dinnertime a sports flavor. Or, if you prefer a newscaster, rather than a sportscaster, approach: "We're standing in the kitchen of the Smith family, waiting eagerly for the first reports of dinner." At this point, thrust the "microphone" toward your youngster and ask him or her to describe how they feel to be part of this momentous occasion.

It may not be NBC, but combining sports- and newscasting with dinnertime makes for hungry headlines!

CATEGORY
In the Kitchen

24

Fresh Off the Press

If your local supermarket offers weekly circulars, then you and your child have the makings of some appealing games. Have your child pick up a circular at the store (or bring one from home), and ask him or her to find: all the fruits, the red items, the foods with seeds, the vegetables with leaves, and so on.

Your older child can use the circular to practice some supermarket math. You might ask, "What would it cost if we bought three jars of peanut butter and four cans of tuna?" Or, "If we had ten dollars, would we have enough money to buy a package of chicken, a bunch of broccoli, and two boxes of macaroni?"

Your kids can also match sale items from the circular with the real things on the shelves. If coupons are available, your children can be responsible for pointing them out to you. That may result in some unexpected purchases, though; you probably didn't expect to buy two jars of anchovy paste and get one free!

REQUIRED
• store circular

CATEGORY
Out and About

Gimme Shelter

25

What better cure for cabin fever than having your child build his or her own cabin using the couch and some blankets?

For basic couch cabin construction, have your child stand the cushions on end, at angles to each other. Adding a blanket for a roof makes the rustic home ready for occupancy. If a bigger cabin for two or more kids is needed, have the troop use chairs as "poles" for hanging blankets or large towels. Also, a couple of small tables set side by side with a blanket or beach towel draped over them make a wonderful tunnel-like entrance that can lead to the "main living area."

Once the shelter is ready, details can be added to the homestead. A circle of blocks with a few sheets of crumpled red and orange paper make an ideal campfire. Small pillows can serve as rock seats. Suggest using a floor lamp or table leg to tether a weary steed.

If the couch house is big enough for you, you might find that there are lots of advantages to living simply.

REQUIRED
- couch cushions and pillows
- blankets or large towels
- chairs and small tables
- blocks
- red and orange paper

CATEGORY
At Home

26

⚠ adult
supervision

Go Boating

Don't have time to visit the yacht club because you have to cook dinner tonight? Then bring the club into your kitchen with a miniature "dishpan regatta."

You and your kids can easily make boats and catamarans with common household items. To make a sailboat, insert a toothpick into a cork near one end (the mast). Then cut out an appropriately sized triangular sail from the plastic liner of a cereal or cracker box and tape it onto the mast. Now cut a slit (your job) into the opposite side of the cork (the bottom) and insert a dime about an eighth of an inch or deep enough so that it will stay in place. The dime will keep the boat upright in the water.

Place the boats in a dishpan filled with water, and provide your captains with straws so they can blow their craft around the water. With a bit of practice they'll be able to do fancy turns or figure eights, or maybe even set a "World Dishpan Record!"

REQUIRED
- corks
- toothpicks
- plastic liner from cereal/ cracker boxes
- tape
- dimes
- dishpan or large baking pan

CATEGORY
In the Kitchen

Godzilla Returns (Again)

Here's a winning activity for sci-fi fans that involves creating a monster film right in your living room. Try these production and prop tips and ideas to get started:

- Paper-bag space helmets are easy to make. The monster can wear a decorated paper-bag mask. Tape on toilet paper tubes to create a high-tech look.

- Couch cushions arranged in a tunnel make great caves for beasts to emerge from.

- For low-budget special effects, pause the camera, have all the actors freeze in place, then have the monster join the scene (appearing out of thin air) before restarting the camera.

- A cityscape can be created out of empty boxes, which will collapse dramatically when the monster stomps on them.

- A paper plate covered with aluminum foil makes a great flying saucer.

Recommend experimenting with different story ideas: For example, a scary visitor from another planet may turn out to be a good buddy after obvious (and amusing) language difficulties are overcome and fears are put aside.

REQUIRED
- video camera or smart phone
- paper bags and toilet paper tubes
- art supplies
- cardboard boxes
- aluminum foil
- paper plate
- couch cushions

CATEGORY
At Home

28

Great Wiper Ensemble

REQUIRED
• your time only

Maybe you can't fit a twelve-piece orchestra in your car, but you can certainly enjoy the next-best thing: a set of windshield wipers!

Let the rhythm of the windshield wipers set the pace for a stellar family performance. Each of the passengers chooses a sound: hand clapping, toe tapping, box thumping, or vocalizing a syllable such as "ah," "eee," or "hoo." You assign each person a time and frequency to make the sound (based on the windshield wipers' rhythm; for example, a "musician" might clap in time to each windshield-wiper beat or tap his or her toe on every other beat).

Each person practices making his or her sound alone; then the whole family performs together. A designated "musician" begins by making a sound. At the signal, the next player jumps in, then the next, and so on, until the entire ensemble is "making music." See how long the family chorus can keep time to the windshield wipers (when players get confused, simply stop the "music" and begin again).

With practice (and a bit of rain), your family members may soon have your car sounding like Symphony Hall!

CATEGORY
On the Road

Guess That Sound

Shhh, what's that sound? You and your child will certainly enjoy finding out. Close your eyes or turn your back, and have your child find an item (either in the same room or another part of your home), then retrieve it. For younger children, you might want to preselect some unbreakable, kid-safe objects from which to choose. Your child then uses the item to make a sound, and you have to guess what the object is.

If you're stumped, ask for hints. For example, if your child is tapping the floor with your brown boots, he or she might say, "This is a sound that people sometimes make when they're walking." And if you need another clue, your child can add, "But you'd only hear this when it's snowing." Still haven't guessed it? Your child might then elaborate, "This came from your shoebox, and it matches your new jacket." Aha, you finally guessed it!

Then it's your child's turn: You choose an object and have your child guess what the sound is. For something that might sound really alien to him or her, how about the sound of running water (as in brushing teeth)?

REQUIRED
- common household items

CATEGORY
At Home

30 Hat Potato

Here's a neat takeoff on "hot potato" that's fun for younger kids. To begin the game, each child needs a hat. Next, make up ten to fifteen "Hat Potato" slips (small pieces of paper with simple but silly instructions written on them, such as "Hop on one foot and quack like a duck" or "Slither like a snake"). Select one of the hats to be the "Hat Potato" and flipping the instructions over, tape the slips of paper to the outside of the hat (or write the instructions on the back side of sticky notes).

REQUIRED
• play or real hats
• writing supplies
• tape
• radio or other audio device

OPTIONAL
• sticky notes

Have the children sit sideways in a circle on the floor so that each child faces the back of the person's head in front of him or her. Each child also wears a hat, one of them being the "Hat Potato." Once the kids are in place, turn on some music; have each of them remove their hat and place it on the head of the child in front of them. This hat passing continues until you stop the music; whoever has the "Hat Potato" on their head takes one slip of paper from it and follows the directions on it (you or an older sibling can help pre-readers).

When the laughter stops, start the music + the hat passing again.

CATEGORY
At Home

Hat Trimming

In the children's book, *Jenny's Hat*, by Ezra Jack Keats, a child is feeling bad about her plain old hat. But her bird friends come to the rescue with decorations such as a valentine, flowers, and even a bird's nest.

Even if your child doesn't have fine-feathered friends, he or she can construct a great hat. Take a strip of clear adhesive covering and wrap it around the top of your child's favorite hat, sticky side out. You might have to hold the covering paper in place with double-stick tape.

Now your child can festoon his or her hat by placing the following types of decorations on the adhesive covering: cutouts of flowers, people, animals, cars, and geometric shapes; pictures from magazines, postcards, and junk mail; cotton balls; and anything else that will make for lively headgear decorations.

With a hat like this, your child is sure to turn some heads.

REQUIRED
- hat
- clear adhesive covering
- art supplies
- magazines and other picture sources
- recycled materials

CATEGORY
At Home

32

Heads Up

A popular song once pointed out that "one man's ceiling is another man's floor." In this drawing game, one person's smile may well be another's eyebrows—with hilarious results!

Two people work together to create this top-to-bottom drawing of a person's face. To start, have the two artists sit facing each other with a sheet of paper between them. Draw a large oval on the page so that the long dimension runs from one artist to the other, then have children take turns adding facial features.

Because each child's view is upside-down in relation to the other artist's, the features added will take on a different meaning for each child. If one draws a mouth, for example, it may become frown lines from the other child's perspective. In the same way, eyebrows that one child draws could look like bags under the eyes of the other's face. By the time they have completed their drawing, your children will have created two completely different faces. Who knows which is right-side up?

REQUIRED
• drawing supplies

CATEGORY
Anytime, Anyplace

Hotel Counts

If your trip includes a stay at a hotel, here's something that turns exploring your surroundings into a fun activity. Set out with your kids in the spirit of exploration to find or count the following kinds of items. (Note: This activity is not intended to be done without supervision.)

- Everything that contains the hotel's logo, from towels to insignias on uniforms

- The number of drinking fountains

- The number of ice machines

- The highest room number

- The number of "Do Not Disturb" signs on doorknobs

- The number of exit signs

- The number of plants in the lobby

- The number of hotel employees in the lobby at any one time

- The number of people who come to the front desk every 5 minutes

When you finish this activity, you might want to send the results to the corporate offices. They'd probably appreciate having a group of experts on tap!

REQUIRED
- your time only

CATEGORY
On the Road

34

How Long Before. . .?

REQUIRED
• your time only

Most of the suspense in a kitchen centers around the age-old question: "When's dinner?" Here's a neat way to inject a little anticipation into cooking time, good for one child or a group of hungry kitchen kids.

To play, your child picks a kitchen object (the spatula, the slotted spoon, or the small saucepan, for example). Then, he or she tracks how much time passes before you use it. Or, if your kitchen has tile floors, your child can choose a particular tile and then see how long it is before you step on it.

If more than one child is playing, each one chooses an object. The winner can either be the person who correctly picks the first or last object actually used.

With this activity, your cooking will get more attention than you ever imagined possible. And your kids will be glued to the edge of their seats!

CATEGORY
In the Kitchen

Humdinger

Making music is one of the best ways we have of passing the time. Here are some suggestions for using singing to create your own games.

If you have younger kids with you, take turns humming a song and see who can guess the name. Stick to old favorites like "This Old Man." During special holidays, try humming seasonal tunes.

Another musical game—"song charades"— doesn't involve humming or singing at all. One player silently acts out a song, while the others try to guess what it is. An alternative way to guess is to hum the tune instead of saying the answer.

Other variations include clapping out a tune, and humming a song in a monotone.

Finally, do a "Johnny-One-Note" hum-along. To play, choose a song. Each person hums a single note in turn, around and around until the whole song is sung. Kind of makes you feel like you're part of a human pipe organ!

REQUIRED
• your time only

CATEGORY
Anytime, Anyplace

36

Indoor Treasure Hunts

Even Sherlock Holmes had to start somewhere en route to becoming a great detective. Here's how to get your child started on the road to finding clues that lead to great treasures.

As in the traditional treasure hunt, the idea is to place clues around the house, with the first clue leading your child to the second, the second to the third, and so on, until he or she reaches the treasure (a cookie or appropriate treat, perhaps).

REQUIRED
• writing supplies

OPTIONAL
• cookie or treat

The twist here is to rename the rooms of the house and devise appropriate clues. For instance, the kitchen might be named the North Pole, and a clue leading to the refrigerator might read, "Find the paper stuck to the giant iceberg of the North Pole." Younger children can join in the fun by having older kids read and interpret the clues.

Play this a sufficient number of times and you might just launch your child's professional detective career.

CATEGORY
At Home

In-Flight Map Game Pack

With a little imagination and a pencil, the route map in your complimentary airline magazine can become a whole package of games and puzzles. Try engaging your child with these games:

Connect the dots. Trace selected route lines to create a picture of an animal, person, or thing.

How NOT to get there. Devise the longest route imaginable to travel from one city to another.

Alphabet tally. Count all the places on the map whose names begin with the same letter.

You can't get there from here. Find the two cities that would require the most flight changes to get from one to the other.

By the way, did you know that the worst way to get from Bali to Oslo is by way of Yap, Chuuk, Tegucigalpa, and Cleveland?

REQUIRED
- complimentary airline magazine
- writing supplies

CATEGORY
On the Road

38

Invisible Kids

What if your children were suddenly heard but not seen because they were invisible? Ask how they would:

Enjoy the perks of being invisible. What would your kids do that visible kids can't? Would they still take baths? Would they get sneak previews of museum exhibits off-limits to the public?

Conduct themselves in public. What pleasant mischief would they get themselves into? Perhaps they'd tickle people waiting in line in stores or adjust people's hats as they rode a bus.

Get people's attention politely and without scaring them. If your kids sat down, how would they let people know "this seat is taken?" How would your children let teachers know when they wanted to be called on? How would your kids greet their friends and initiate conversations?

Once your kids have thought about what it might be like to be invisible, pose this question: If you could be heard but not seen, would you?

REQUIRED
• your time only

CATEGORY
Anytime, Anyplace

It's Great to Be . . .

Here's how you can help your child understand that any age is a great age to be.

Give your child three or four sheets of paper, a pencil, and verbal instructions to write his or her current age at the top of the first page. On subsequent pages, your child can write some of the important ages he or she has been (a ten-year-old might have pages entitled "ten," "six," "two," and "newborn").

Then ask your child to make a list of all the best things about being each of those ages. He or she can include abilities, privileges, events, hopes and ambitions, and so on. For example, on the "newborn" page, your child might list: "Met my family," "Learned new things all the time," etc. Under "two," he or she might write: "Learned to run," "Made my first friends," "Visited Grandma," and so on.

When your child is finished writing, staple the pages together and put them in a safe place. He or she can add to it periodically upon discovering the best things about being an older kid.

REQUIRED
• writing supplies
• stapler

CATEGORY
Anytime, Anyplace

40

Kitchen Bowling and Other Sports

A soft foam or rubber ball is just the thing to get a few kitchen games off and rolling, and entertain you and your kids while you cook.

Have your kids set up ten paper cups (preferably recycled) on the floor. Mark a line with a piece of masking tape, or designate a certain line between floor tiles. Your kids stand behind the line and roll the ball at the cups. Older kids can keep score.

REQUIRED
- foam or soft rubber ball
- paper cups
- plastic pitcher
- wrapping paper tube

With a few modifications, the bowling alley becomes a giant arcade game—simply arrange the cups to form an alley, with one or two slightly extending into the path. The goal is to try to roll the ball through the alley without touching a cup.

And when your kids are done with the bowling and arcade games, suggest a little putting practice to build up a good appetite. Set a plastic pitcher on its side on the floor and provide a wrapping paper tube. Your kids can take turns using the tube as a putter and the pitcher as the hole.

CATEGORY
In the Kitchen

Label Master

41

Have you ever read a food label? All you get is the percentage of fat and vitamins and the like. The really good information, like the percentage of yumminess, is nowhere to be found.

Your kids can remedy that situation—and stay busy while you work—by creating their own food labels for all sorts of packaged foods in your kitchen. All they need are a few colored markers or crayons, paper, and transparent tape.

Even kids too young to write can join in the fun by decorating labels with pictures. Kids who have writing skills can invent their own ingredients that go into the cereal, the soup, and the crackers (high in cement and tree bark, and a great source of Vitamin X23).

Have your kids affix the labels to the food packages with tape—the next time someone goes into the pantry for a snack, they might be relieved to learn that their favorite chips are 100 percent lightning- and snow-free!

REQUIRED
• art supplies
• packaged foods

CATEGORY
In the Kitchen

42

Log Those Plates!

How can you remember the most unusual license plates that you pass on the road? By preserving them in a logbook, of course.

To make a log, use a notebook or sheets of paper that can later be stapled together. At the top of each page write the time span of each license-watch period (say 8:15 to 8:30 A.M.) and the watch category (in this case, out-of-state license plates).

REQUIRED
• writing supplies

You and your co-travelers scout the road and look for out-of-state license plates. The designated log keeper then makes a list of the license plates as they are spotted.

Your family can also watch for and log other license-plate features including colors, slogans, and letters and digits (for example, how many license plates can you find that contain the letter W?).

You can reserve a special section in your logbook for vanity plates. See who can find the funniest, most original, or most cryptic in a given time period. Then log the ultimate challenge: the number of license plates each family member can memorize in one sitting.

CATEGORY
On the Road

Macaroni Math

Let's see, how does that old song go? "Stuck a feather in his cap and called it vermicelli." We may be confused about "Yankee Doodle," but your kids won't be mixed up about addition or subtraction when they use macaroni noodles to do some math.

Give your child some noodles (gear the number of noodles to your child's math level) and a placemat or dish. Then, as you're cooking, present your child with simple arithmetic problems. You might, for example, say: "How much is two plus four?" To find the answer, your child counts out the appropriate number of noodles and tells you what the total is.

Older children who can handle larger numbers can use different-colored noodles to calculate higher totals. Each color can represent a different amount: yellows are ones, reds are tens, greens are hundreds, etc. . Your child can line up the noodles in columns and add or subtract the appropriate amounts.

Entertaining your kids while you cook isn't so hard. You just have to make every noodle count!

REQUIRED
- macaroni noodles
- placemat or dish

CATEGORY
In the Kitchen

44 Magical Mystery Machine

- boxes
- recycled household materials
- magazines and other photo sources
- art supplies
- tape and nontoxic glue

As this activity will prove, imagination is the real mother of invention.

Gather up an assortment of art supplies, odds and ends, lids, spools, foil, and shoeboxes, and have your child build an imaginary machine (one that turns spinach into ice cream, sounds an alarm when baby brother enters the room, or polishes the cat's claws). Your child can start with a plain shoebox and add plastic lids and paper arrows for dials, cardboard tubes for feeding in "raw material," and yarn for "drive belts." Encourage the inventor to decide on a purpose for every piece he or she puts on the machine. Suggest decorating the devices with tempera paint, markers, recycled foil, and pictures cut out of magazines, junk mail, catalogs, and so on.

Later, say after dinner, have your child make a presentation to the rest of the family, explaining in detail what the gadget does and how it works.

Just one question: Does the cat get to pick which color claw polish she wants?

CATEGORY
At Home

Make an Ad

Are you and your child tired of seeing the same old newspaper and magazine ads? Here's how to take revenge on the advertising pros.

Browse through newspapers and magazines, then clip photos as well as bits and pieces of copy from ads, reassembling them into wacky hybrids that parody or spoof the originals. Add a wild headline (the more incongruous the better), then affix all the pieces with glue or double-stick tape to a sheet of paper or poster board.

When you and your child have finished your "ad campaigns," pass the ads back and forth or take turns reading the headlines and text aloud, seeing who can suppress their giggles the longest. If a group is playing, each participant can stand up and do a dramatic reading of his or her ad.

Twenty percent off the price of ear polish that three out of four city council members recommend? Sounds great to us. . . .

REQUIRED
- magazines
- newspapers and other photo and text sources
- double-stick tape or nontoxic glue
- paper or poster board
- scissors
- writing supplies

CATEGORY
At Home

46

Make-Before-You-Go Card Game Board

Simple games like concentration are a great way for your kids to pass the time but are difficult to play in a car, train, or plane. Here's a simple portable game board to make before you go (see illustration).

To make the board, first cut a ten-inch-square piece of cardboard. Then cut four 10 x 3 3/4 inch strips of construction paper and cover one side with clear adhesive covering. Fold the strips lengthwise with the adhesive covering on the outside, so that one side measures 2 1/2 inches and the other 1 1/4 inches. Next, glue the 2 1/2-inch side to the cardboard. Staple through both sides of the strips and the cardboard at 2-inch intervals to form five pockets on each strip.

To make playing cards, have your children draw pairs of objects that they anticipate seeing on your trip on the top half of thirty or so 1 1/2 x 2 1/4 inch pieces of thin cardboard. Or have them find pairs of pictures in magazines and glue them onto the upper portions of the cards. Then have them write each letter of the alphabet on one end of the other side of the card; if you have extra cards, repeat the vowels. You can cover the cards with clear adhesive covering if you wish. When the preparation is done, pack everything up in a paper or plastic bag, and you're ready to roll.

REQUIRED
- cardboard
- thin cardboard
- construction paper
- clear adhesive covering
- glue
- stapler
- scissors
- ruler
- magazines
- paper or plastic bag

CATEGORY
At Home

Make-Before-You-Go Mileage Bags

Here's a twist on the time-honored practice of giving kids special snacks, small toys, and other diversions as you make your way down the highway: "mileage bags," or goodie bags, dispersed after you have traveled certain predetermined distances.

Have your children help decorate the mileage bags (paper lunch bags, actually). Then, together, decide the distance between goodie distributions, and label the bags accordingly. If, for example, you plan to travel 420 miles and you want to make up five bags, you could have your children label them 70, 140, 210, 280, and 350 miles.

Next, fill the bags with surprises. You can include snacks, small books, small toys, even coupons good for frozen yogurt at the next rest stop. When you're traveling, you'll be all set to give your kids the bags at the designated distances (you can have your children watch highway signs so they can keep track of the miles themselves).

Your kids will be glad to know that while it's twenty miles to the next rest stop, it's only five miles to the next mileage bag!

REQUIRED
- paper lunch bags
- art supplies
- snacks
- small books and toys
- homemade coupons

CATEGORY
At Home

48 Make-Before-You-Go Swiss Army Notebook

It's a paper holder, a playing board, a felt board, a writing surface, a traveling file, and more! To make a "Swiss Army Notebook," add the following to a smooth-surfaced three-ring binder:

Paper supplies. Include an ample supply of paper: lined, blank, graph, and so on.

Writing and drawing supplies. Punch three holes in a clasp envelope or self-sealing plastic bag to hold pens, pencils, crayons, and markers.

Felt board. Glue a piece of felt to the back of the notebook and cut shapes out of felt scraps to make designs. Store the shapes in an envelope.

Clipboard. Attach a bulldog clip to the top of the front cover of the notebook.

Keepsake holders. Add some empty envelopes to store ticket stubs, brochures, and guides.

You may find that this organizer is so handy you'll want one for yourself!

REQUIRED
- three-ring binder
- clasp envelope or self-sealing plastic bag
- envelopes
- paper
- writing and drawing supplies
- felt
- bulldog clip

CATEGORY
At Home

Make-Believe on the Range

Who's cooking at your house? Your kids with their own stove, that's who.

Take an empty large carton, tape both ends closed, and make a door by drawing a square on the front of the box, then cutting the square on three sides so that it swings open (your job).

Next, your kids can trace circles above the door using the narrow end of small paper cups. Cut out the circles. Your kids then insert the bottoms of the cups through the holes from inside the box—presto, instant dials. Your kids can draw designs on the dials to match those on your stove or oven.

Your kids can also easily make burners on the top of the stove by tracing circles around different-sized pan lids. Or they may want to glue paper plates on top of the box—that is, stove.

Your kids are really cooking now!

REQUIRED
- large carton
- paper cups
- paper plates
- tape
- art supplies

CATEGORY
At Home

50

Modern Conveniences

So your kids are tired of waiting and are getting bored? Just have them look around at all the exciting things that have interesting imaginary histories.

Take that doorknob over there. Who invented it? And when? Ask your resident expert questions like "Why were doorknobs necessary?" "What did people do without them?" "What was the person's name who came up with the idea?" "What kind of commotion did the invention make in the town where the inventor lived?" and so on.

REQUIRED
• your time only

You can also turn the session into a role-play activity, during which you take the position of a naysayer. "What? Impossible! Doorknobs will forever alter the shape of human hands!!!"

You can play this game with just about anything from concrete and glass to shoelaces and ballpoint pens. All of the things you take for granted are grist for the expert's mill. For that matter, what is the story behind the old gristmill?

CATEGORY
Anytime, Anyplace

More Than Meets the Eye

A young person with lots of great ideas for fun, Sarah, told us that a terrific way to entertain yourself is to describe the world to an imaginary friend. Play this game in your kitchen or anyplace else.

Ask your child to imagine that a friend from another time or planet has come to visit, and is quite baffled by all of the gadgets and appliances in your kitchen. Your child's job is to explain each item—what it does and how it works. You play the part of the onlooker, prompting your child to explain things that both of you take for granted.

For example, you might point to the can opener and ask your child to explain what it is. After your child identifies it, see if he or she can describe how the gear mechanism works. Or the refrigerator—just what makes it cold? And that funny box on the counter (the microwave)—what's the magic behind it?

When you finish this game you'll probably have answers to those big questions you've been wondering about all these years—like how the telephone knows it's time to ring right when you sit down to dinner.

REQUIRED
• your time only

CATEGORY
Anytime, Anyplace

52

⚠ small parts

Muffin Tin Toss

When you break out the muffin tins for this game, your kids will probably expect something special for dessert. You can give them something just as yummy: a great way to entertain themselves before mealtime.

Kids set the muffin tins on the floor and assign points for each cup. The players take turns tossing an object into the tins, such as beans, dried macaroni, or pennies. (Small objects aren't appropriate for small kids.) If your kids are old enough to use coin math in the game, they can make "heads" worth a single score, while "tails" is worth double the amount.

As a variation, the players can toss with their eyes closed. They can also write a number on scraps of colored paper, one for each cup in the tin. Numbers on the green scraps might be positive, while those on the red scraps are to be subtracted from the score.

REQUIRED
• muffin tins
• small household objects

OPTIONAL
• colored paper
• writting supplies

CATEGORY
At Home

Museum Scavenger Hunt

53

If you're looking for ways to make museum trips more exciting for your kids, give this activity a try.

First, plan your scavenger hunt by visiting the museum's Web site before you go or by stopping by the information desk once you arrive and picking up any maps and brochures about the exhibition. Look over the materials together and devise a list of five to ten very specific things to hunt for. In a natural-history museum, these could include the T-rex skull, the Atlantic puffin, the trilobite diorama, gypsum needles, and the Audubon print of a great egret; in an art museum, the list could include a painting of a vase of flowers and a pair of gloves on a table, a sculpture of a child with a bird, a mask from the Aleutian Eskimos, a small gold Mayan figure, a round fan, or "uchiwa," from Japan, and a sculpture of a ballerina with a real net skirt.

Once you've compiled your list, set off for the exhibits. You can either work together to find all of the items, or you can break into teams (each with an adult) with specific assignments.

Perhaps you'll even find a painting of a man who looks like Uncle Fred!

REQUIRED
• complimentary museum exhibit maps and brochures

CATEGORY
On the Road

54

My Strangest Case

REQUIRED
• your time only

Here's a great way to pass some time in a waiting room—and, if it happens to be the waiting room of the doctor or dentist, defuse a little anxiety.

Take turns imagining that you're the doctor or dentist, and that you're describing the strangest case of the day, like the person who swallowed a tuba and, every time he exhaled, he sounded like a foghorn. Perhaps, as a dentist, you've seen a young fellow who brushed his teeth with white glue by mistake and couldn't open his mouth.

This activity works well in any waiting room situation. Perhaps you're waiting for an oil change or car repair; you and your child can take turns pretending you're the mechanic and describing oddities such as the person who locked an egg-salad sandwich in the glove compartment and lost the key.

You can also play this game by describing an imaginary problem and inviting your child to describe its outcome. You're bound to get some interesting answers. Perhaps the person who swallowed the tuba got a new job with the Coast Guard!

CATEGORY
Out and About

Mystery Story

Can you and your child co-author a great story knowing only a minimum of what the other is plotting? Find out with this activity.

Set up a "recording studio" (if possible, choose a room with a door) by placing a recording device (MP3 player, smartphone, or memo recorder) on a table or desk. Have your child leave the room, then record the title and the first couple of lines of your story. When you reach a "cliffhanger" (an exciting spot in the narrative or simply the word "and"), hit the stop button and ask your child to come back into the room. Tell him or her the last five words of your recording, then leave the room. Your child then records a couple of lines to the story and tells you his or her last five words as you switch roles. Continue in this fashion until the story reaches a conclusion.

REQUIRED
• recording device (MP3 player, smartphone, or memo recorder)

When the narrative is complete, play back the tape with the two of you in the room. You're bound to get a few chuckles as the tale takes some strange twists and turns.

CATEGORY
At Home

56 Navigator's Hat

Even if your children aren't old enough to drive, they can still help get you to your destination. Make (or select) a special hat before you leave home. Then have your kids take turns wearing the hat and performing the following navigator duties:

Sign spotter. If you're looking for a particular town or exit, or the next rest area, have the navigator watch for signs.

Map travel recorder. The navigator traces your route on a map with a highlighter pen, adding markers in the appropriate places to indicate all of your stops.

Travel updater. Have your navigator periodically report which direction you're heading in, how far you've gone, and how many miles you have to travel until the next stop.

And, of course, when you come to a crossroads and don't have a clue as to where you are, the navigator can help you guess which way to go next!

REQUIRED
- paper
- drawing supplies
- road map
- hat

CATEGORY
On the Road

No "Ors," "Ands," (or) "Buts"

57

Want to hear a great story? Then create one with your child, a word at a time.

Have your child say, write, or type any word to begin the tale. Then you add a word, and your child adds another, until the first sentence is finished. This cooperative writing approach continues until the story comes to a conclusion. It may or may not be the ending you had envisioned, but that's the whole point: You never know what direction the tale will take when you and your child become co-authors.

REQUIRED
• writing supplies

Once you've gotten the hang of co-writing a story in this fashion, up the ante by introducing a new rule: No one can use the words "or," "and," or "but." That's a lot more difficult than it sounds. Take turns inventing new rules, too, just to keep each other on your toes.

Gee, that's going to be tough when you can only use words less than five letters long . . . .

CATEGORY
At Home

58 Noah's Noodle Maze

REQUIRED
• cooked
  spaghetti
  noodles

Do your kids like puzzles? One of the favorite
diversions around our house is solving mazes.
Your child can build his or her own, right in the
kitchen.

This activity is perfect if you're making spaghetti,
because your kids will use cooked spaghetti
noodles to make their maze. Your child takes
some noodles and arranges them so that there's
one path from beginning to end, cutting them as
needed. If your puzzle-maker wants to get fancy,
he or she can create the maze on a plate—a
circular maze is sure to pose some interesting
problems. When the maze is ready, take a break
from your cooking, set the timer, and see if you
can find your way from beginning to end before
the buzzer goes off, running a chopstick along
the noodle pathways.

This might be the only puzzle in your house
that, after solving it, you can douse with a little
sauce and eat!

CATEGORY
In the Kitchen

Noah's Noodle Stamps and Brushes

The noodle is the artist's best friend, as our son, Noah, once pointed out to us while we boiled a pot of ziti. Here's how to prove it.

Provide an assortment of uncooked small noodles, such as ziti, corkscrew, radiatore, rigatoni, and penne. Your child presses one end onto a washable stamp pad, or dips it in a thin layer of tempera paint, then presses the inked or painted end onto a piece of paper to create scenes, people, abstract art, or even write messages in "noodlese."

Another way to do noodle painting is to make a "brush" ahead of time by gluing noodles of varying lengths across two Popsicle sticks (like a segment of picket fence, with the Popsicle sticks serving as rails and the noodles as pickets). Before the glue sets, press a piece of cardboard along the bottoms of the noodles so they're flush. Let the noodles dry, then glue two Popsicle sticks perpendicular to the "fence rails"; this is the handle. When that's dried, dip the "brush" into tempera paint and get set for some exciting art.

Hey, Noah, THAT'S using your noodle!

REQUIRED
- uncooked noodles
- washable ink pad or tempera paint
- four popsicle sticks
- nontoxic glue
- paper

CATEGORY
In the Kitchen

60 Number Hunt

REQUIRED
• your time only

Do you notice the numbers you see throughout the day, especially in your own kitchen? Chances are, your kids usually don't. Here's a simple game that opens their eyes and gives them a start on basic number skills.

The object of the game is to find all of the numbers that are visible in the kitchen; everything's fair game. The clock and measuring cups are obvious. Cereal box labels and the like are subtler.

If several children play, they can work together as a team, trying to create the highest value by adding up numbers from one object. (Hint: Many packaged foods have a customer service telephone number somewhere on the label—that will bring up the totals.) For an added challenge, suggest that players must find numbers in consecutive order.

So, what's the biggest number in your kitchen today?

CATEGORY
In the Kitchen

Off-the-Cuff

It takes a good orator to make an excellent speech on an important topic. But it takes a great orator—like your child—to give an extemporaneous speech about practically anything!

When you have some extra time, and your child is in a talkative mood, point to any object. Then have your child make a speech about it. You might specify a time limit—say, three minutes—during which your speech maker can talk about the object's real or fictional history, who invented it, what earlier versions looked like, how it was first used, how it's used today, how it might be improved or adapted in the future, and so on.

For a real challenge, point to an obscure object such as the metal ring at the end of a pencil, the plastic ends on a shoelace, or the T-shaped piece of plastic that holds a tag on a new item of clothing. See whether your child can make a full-length speech on the subject. Perhaps he or she can even tell you what the tagholder is really called!

REQUIRED
• your time only

CATEGORY
Anytime, Anyplace

62

62

adult
supervision

REQUIRED
- paper plates or plastic lids
- tape or nontoxic glue
- art supplies
- scissors

Oversized Homemade Checkers

Why settle for conventionally sized checkers when your kids can create a giant checker set that's as much fun to make as it is to play with?

To start, gather twenty-four paper plates or plastic lids and have your children decorate them so that they have two sets of twelve "checkers" each. (If you use plastic lids, you'll probably need to glue on circles of paper to make decorating easier.) Have the kids decorate the bottoms of the playing pieces with a distinctive design (like a crown or a royal face) so that a piece can be flipped over to show that it is a "king."

Next, have your children cut sixty-four squares of paper (thirty-two each of two colors) slightly larger than the playing pieces; you might need to draw cutting lines for them. They should then place the squares on the floor in an eight-by-eight square grid with colors alternating and tape the edges together as they go.

Now clear your room; you're dealing with major-league games!

CATEGORY
At Home

Offline Activities You Can Do with Your Child

Pass the Exits

What can travelers do with exit signs besides pass them on the road? Why, remember them, of course!

Appoint a passenger to read and write down exit signs, including names and numbers, as they appear. (This works best with a series of exit signs in close proximity.) Players see whether they can remember and recite the signs—in reverse order.

For example, let's say you've passed three signs. The first player recites the list from memory (for example, "exit 16, Wilson City; exit 15, Clearfield; exit 14, Riverdale"). After passing the next sign, the second player adds, "exit 17, South Sunset," and then recites the other three signs. The next player adds the new sign and recites the other four, and so on, until players can no longer remember the whole list.

Map readers can try this variation. One person identifies the next three exits on the map. Players then memorize the exit names and numbers, and try to recall them before the exit sign appears. That's one great way to put your astounding memory on the map!

REQUIRED
- writing supplies
- road map

CATEGORY
On the Road

64 Patterns

REQUIRED
• writing supplies

Does your child like making and finding patterns? If so, he or she will enjoy this pattern puzzle. It's easy to do, and the results are never the same twice.

Begin the puzzle by drawing a series of simple geometrical shapes on a sheet of paper to create a repetitive pattern. The more shapes you use, the more complicated the pattern can become. It can be as simple as:

l o l o l o l o l o

or something more elaborate, like:

o o + l o o + l

Now see if your child can figure out the pattern and continue it. For a more challenging puzzle, you and your child can create a two-dimensional pattern, such as:

o o

o   o

o   o

o o

CATEGORY
Anytime, Anyplace

After a while, you and your child will certainly notice another pattern developing: that time flies when you're having fun!

People Food

Here's a neat way to keep your child entertained—and stimulate his or her creativity during busy cooking sessions.

The idea is for your child to draw a person using different kinds of food for various body parts. A head of lettuce, for instance, could become a person's head. Carrot or celery sticks could become legs, and radish slices could serve as eyes. Your child can even make up stories that go along with his or her food people.

As an alternative to drawing, kids can cut pictures of food out of circulars, magazines, and newspapers, then arrange and glue them into people shapes. They can also arrange them into animals—a can of dog food standing on four dog biscuits would make for an interesting canine creature.

Provide enough circulars, and your kids will have a whole town's worth of food people out walking their food dogs and cats!

REQUIRED
• art supplies

OPTIONAL
• food circulars, magazines or newspapers

CATEGORY
In the Kitchen

66 Pin the Food on the Plate

REQUIRED
- art supplies
- paper plate
- food circulars or magazine
- tape
- magnetic letters (for variation)

If you're making a special birthday meal, this game can be played by several kids at once. Not only does it give them something to do while you cook, but it adds to the "party" atmosphere.

The game is modeled after "Pin the Tail on the Donkey." To play, your kids cut out pictures of food from grocery ads, food circulars, or magazines. Then they stick a small loop of tape to the back of each picture. Finally, they attach a paper plate to the refrigerator with tape. Now they're ready to play.

Each player takes a food picture, closes his or her eyes, then tries to place that picture on the plate. After all the pictures have been placed, kids can have fun talking about the crazy meal they concocted.

A quick alternative to this game, if you have a fridge covered with magnetic letters, is to dump the letters in a hat, have kids close their eyes, pick letters, and place them on the fridge. What words can they make from the jumbled letters? Hey, that spells fun!

CATEGORY
In the Kitchen

Ping-Pong Potpourri

67

Here are some more quick ideas for using a Ping-Pong ball for kitchen entertainment.

First have your kids try a little warm-up exercise—seeing how long they can bounce a Ping-Pong ball inside a sauce pan. Then see if your kids can bounce a Ping-Pong ball and catch it in a small strainer. Or put the ball into a muffin tin and have the players try to roll the ball from cup to cup.

When everyone's worn out, they can try their hand at "carousel," which entails placing a Ping-Pong ball in a large bowl. The players then take turns rotating the bowl so that the ball rolls along the sides. The faster they turn the bowl, the higher the ball rises on the side. How far and fast can it go without shooting out? NASA calls this exit speed "escape velocity," but these Ping-Pong challenges will more than likely keep your kids happily in the kitchen orbit.

REQUIRED
- saucepans, strainer
- muffin tin
- Ping-Pong ball
- large bowl

CATEGORY
In the Kitchen

68

Repealing Newton's Law

What if it were possible to make anti-gravity machines? Ask your kids how the machines would:

Change the world. Would it be necessary to have elevators or escalators? Or could people simply float up inside tubes to whatever floor they wanted to go and grab hold of "floor handles?" How about anti-gravity boots; perhaps runners could simply "anti-grav" hop over obstacles.

REQUIRED
• your time only

Lead to new forms of entertainment. Maybe we'd see the first "Anti-Gravity Arena," where people bounced off foam ceilings, kind of like reverse bungee jumping. What other kinds of games and thrills can your kids envision?

Avoid misuse of the devices. How could we prevent mishaps, such as people floating off into space, or anti-gravity machines accidentally turning on and disrupting a whole building or community?

Once your kids have thought about these issues, pose this question: Would you want an antigravity machine, if somebody offered to build one for you?

CATEGORY
Anytime, Anyplace

Rosetta Stones

The Rosetta stone enabled eighteenth-century scholars to decipher the hieroglyphics of ancient Egypt by providing "parallel" passages in Greek and Egyptian. You can invent your own Rosetta stones right in your living room, and you won't even need a hammer and chisel.

Take a piece of paper and list all the letters of the alphabet in a column. Next to each letter, place a different geometrical shape, arrow, simple picture, or other visual substitute.

REQUIRED
• writing supplies

Now write out a message using the "graphic alphabet," hand your child the translation sheet, and see if he or she can read the correct words.

And for a hotshot code buster, try this: Leave about three quarters of the letters as they are, but substitute graphics and symbols for the rest. Write out a message in the "hybrid" alphabet and see if your child can crack the code without a translation sheet.

S*!%L ?:"@ \K?"0"?L3

(Which means: Enjoy this activity!)

CATEGORY
Anytime, Anyplace

70 Scrambled Recipes

REQUIRED
- recipes
- writing supplies
- ingredients

They know what it looks like. They know what it tastes like. They can even tell it by the aroma. But do your kids really know what goes into their favorite dish?

Test their food knowledge in a fun way by writing down the ingredients from two recipes, with each ingredient on a separate strip of paper. Then tell your kids what the finished dishes are supposed to be. The object is for your kids to separate the ingredients into two piles, one for each recipe. (An alternate version for pre- or early readers is to get out the actual ingredients and see if they can group them by recipes.)

You can increase the challenge in several ways. Try using more than two recipes. Or don't tell your kids the names of the dishes, and see if they can figure out the intended results. Finally, try using similar recipes—cupcakes and banana bread, for example.

Just think, you might be the first to hear about the next great food craze!

CATEGORY
At Home

Sensational Salon

Feel like pampering yourself? Then pay a visit to your home beauty salon, and let your child transform you into a model.

First, have your child furnish his or her beauty parlor with a real or pretend sink (a box), mirror, hair dryer, chairs, etc. Style supplies (clips, ponytail holders, barrettes, headbands, and so on) should also be stocked. Choose your treatment (new style, shampoo, coloring, or whatever); you and your child may find unusual hairstyles to duplicate in magazines or newspapers, or your child can work from your directions or pure imagination.

Of course, your child's beauty services might also extend to other areas, such as manicures, massages, facial masks, and makeup. In fact, why not ask for an entire makeover; with your child's skills, you'll surely be the talk of the town.

REQUIRED
- large cardboard box
- hair dryer and mirror (or make-believe equivalents)
- clips, ponytail holders, barrettes, headbands and other hair accessories

CATEGORY
At Home

72

Shooting Hoops

Here's a way to have some basketball fun in your living room. You don't need a real ball, and you don't need a real hoop; here's how to make your own.

For a ball, use a mesh onion bag filled with wadded-up newspaper and held closed with a rubber band or knotted string. Crumple the newspapers loosely so that they fill up the onion bag.

REQUIRED
- mesh onion bag
- newspapers
- rubber band or string
- large paper bags
- duct tape
- masking tape or string

To make a basket, double up two large paper bags, fold the tops down two to three times in one-inch folds for stiffness, and cut the bottoms out. You may want to add a strip of duct tape around the top for added strength. Then attach the bag to the back of a chair, either with masking tape or string laced through small holes punched in the top strip, and you're ready to begin the game.

Have your children start by seeing how many baskets they can get in ten throws from a fixed line. As their shooting improves, you can have them try more challenging games, like taking a step back after each successful shot they make. With a bit of practice, you'll be ready to take the Living Room Trotters for their debut in the big league.

CATEGORY
At Home

Sign Jumbles

73

The Word Jumbles in the newspaper are one of our favorite ways to pass the time. But you don't need a newspaper to play word games—any sign will do.

To play, just turn your attention to the billboards, store displays, and traffic signs all around you. This is a great way to pass the time while waiting on a bus, or while stopped in traffic.

REQUIRED
• your time only

The object of the game is to see how many words can be made out of the letters on the sign. That stop sign on the corner, for example, contains the word "spot." The marquee outside of the cafe holds the word "face."

When you and your child play together, keep using the same sign to form words until it stumps one of you. The last player to get a word from the sign is the winner.

If you're playing in the car, and you're stopped at a traffic light, keep going until the light turns green—but you'll have to think fast! Just how many words can you get out of that "Pedestrian Crossing" sign, anyway?

CATEGORY
Out and About

74

⚠ adult supervision

Sink or Swim

Cooking and mixing in the kitchen—even a pretend one—are a lot of fun for kids. But where do your kids clean the resulting make-believe mess?

At the play sink, of course. To make the sink, tape both ends of a large carton shut. Then, give your kids a plastic dishpan. After they trace around the top of the pan on one side of the box, cut it out for them (make sure it's slightly smaller than the rim, so the edge will support the rim). Your kids can use the sink dry or with a small amount of water, if you're comfortable with the idea.

To make the faucet and handles, cut three holes, each just wide enough to accommodate a toilet paper or paper towel tube. Insert a paper towel tube for the faucet (middle hole), then cut a wedge from the side of the tube so that you can bend the tube 90°, and tape in place. Insert a toilet paper tube in the holes on either side of the faucet for the handles.

Say, is that a tiger in the kitchen? No, it's just your child impersonating the disposal.

REQUIRED
- large carton
- dishpan or shallow box
- toilet paper or paper towel tubes
- tape
- art supplies

CATEGORY
At Home

Smiling Violations

What if your kids patrolled the highways and byways looking for drivers who hadn't brushed their teeth before getting behind the wheel? They'd probably have a blast!

Here's the next best thing, and your kids don't have to unbuckle their seat belts to do it. Just provide art supplies and paper, and suggest that they make up their own tickets listing silly fines and violations, like the following: fine for driving with a cluttered glove compartment—$5,000; sitting in a standing-only zone—$50; parking on top of a bus—pay seventeen doughnuts; fine for ruining raindrops with windshield wipers—$3 million.

REQUIRED
• art supplies
• paper

Now turn the tables and have your children imagine the kinds of explanations that they might hear if they were to deliver their citations. "Gee, I'm sorry, but the hamsters in the glove compartment were restless," or "But . . . I didn't know I couldn't park my car on the steps." Then there's always this one: "I'm sorry the car was shaking, but we were all just laughing so hard!"

CATEGORY
On the Road

76

Snork!

REQUIRED
• your time only

Here's a great car game that can easily be adjusted to the ages and skills of your children. The point of the game is to have everyone try to guess the identity of an object while one person supplies clues.

To play, one person picks an object that you pass frequently, such as a signpost, a green car, or a gas station. Then, each time the car passes a matching object, he or she calls out "snork" (or some other nonsense word). Everyone else tries to figure out what the item is by looking around when they hear the word "snork" and taking a guess.

To increase the challenge, you can make the object very specific. For example, instead of a green car, the person may pick a green car with four people in it that's traveling in the opposite direction. Then, when someone makes a partially correct guess, the chooser can let the guesser know that the answer is close, but not close enough.

The game can also be varied by picking items that come up more or less frequently. But be careful. If someone picks fence posts, it may all come down to "Snork, snork, snork, snork, snork . . . ."

CATEGORY
On the Road

Soundalikes

Are you and your child hearing double? It's
likely that you will be, once you've discovered
these soundalike word games that you can play
while you're waiting.

First you'll want to explain to your child that
homonyms are two words that sound the
same and are spelled the same, but mean two
different things. Offer your child some examples
of homonyms, such as the words "bat" (a flying
rodent) and "bat" (as in baseball bat). Then ask
your child to come up with other examples of
homonyms.

REQUIRED
• your time only

Still waiting? Then tell your child that
homophones are words that sound the same but
are spelled differently. Provide some examples,
such as "know" and "no," and "whole" and
"hole," and see whether your child can offer
some additional homophones.

Finally, if you have more time to pass, you can
ask your child to invent some "sillophones."
Sillophones are related to homophones, except
that the second soundalike word doesn't exist
until your child creates it. For example, "kid"
and "cid" are sillophones; of course, a cid is an
expert at inventing sillophones!

CATEGORY
Anytime, Anyplace

78

Sounds Like . . .

REQUIRED
• your time only

Onomatopoeia is a term for words that sound like what they are, such as "buzz," "hiss," and "ping." With a little applied theatrics, your kids can probably make a lot of words onomatopoetic.

The word "big," for example, which even though it isn't (big, that is) can certainly sound "big" if said in a deep, resonant voice. And even though "little" is bigger than "big," it won't sound that way if it's said in a soft, squeaky voice.

Make a game out of creating sentences that use words that sound like what they describe, and challenge your kids to use as much tone, volume, and inflection as necessary to take the idea to a silly extreme.

Begin by helping them think of words that genuinely fit the bill: "hiss," "buzz," "crunch," "pop," "sizzle," "bang," and "swish," for example. Then have your children add their own interpretations of how particular words should sound.

So, what's the sound of children pretending to be asleep in the backseat of a car? Snooooooze!

CATEGORY
Anytime, Anyplace

Speedy Word-Guessers

As this activity will show, if you have a pencil and a paper napkin or placemat (or a notepad), you're all set to pass some time until the waiter or waitress takes your order or brings your food to the table. (It's actually a take-off on the old "hangman" game, but in honor of the meal-time spirit, we've done away with the unpleasant metaphor.)

Find a word on a menu, a sign on the wall, a decoration, advertising placard, and so on. Then draw enough blank lines for each letter. The players then take turns offering letters. Write down each correct letter in its proper place. For each incorrect guess, you write down a letter, in sequence, of the restaurant's name.

The object is for your kids to figure out the word before you spell out the entire name of the restaurant. (Note: If the name is exceptionally short or long, you might want to offer another name or word that you'll use to record incorrect guesses.) The person who finishes the round gets to choose the next word, and the game continues—until the food arrives, at which point EVERYONE is a winner!

REQUIRED
- paper napkin, placemat or notepad
- pencil

CATEGORY
Out and About

80 Tabletop Basketball

REQUIRED
- sheet of cardboard
- paper cups
- Ping-Pong balls
- books or other heavy objects

Here's a version of basketball in which someone seven feet tall would be at an extreme disadvantage!

Help your kids create two "nets" (just make one if a single child will be playing). Take a piece of stiff cardboard and cut a hole in it slightly smaller in diameter than the rim of a paper cup (the mouth of the cup should be at least two inches in diameter). Slip the cup through the hole in the cardboard, so that the rim rests on the cardboard. Now place the cardboard at the edge of the table, with the cup extending over the edge. Place a book or other heavy object on the edge of the cardboard so that it doesn't obstruct the cup (see illustration). Repeat the process for the second "net" and place it at the opposite end of the table.

The players then bounce a Ping-Pong ball across the table, trying to land it in each other's net. They can score the game as in traditional basketball, or invent their own system.

You might want to demo your famous hook shot. Wow—what a dunk!

CATEGORY
At Home

Time Travelers

What if it were possible to build a time machine and travel to the past or future? Ask your kids how they would:

Decide which times to visit. Would it be more fun to visit the past or the future? What would they do once they got there?

Explain their presence. Would your kids let other people know that they were time travelers? What would the benefits and the dangers be of telling the truth?

Collect data. What kind of information could your kids gather about other times that would be useful to us now?

Change the past or the future. If your kids could travel through time, what would they change? What might the consequences of those changes be?

Once your kids have thought about what it might be like to travel through time, pose this question: Would you want to time travel, if it were really possible? Why or why not?

REQUIRED
• your time only

CATEGORY
Anytime, Anyplace

82 Trailblazers

REQUIRED
- socks
- writing supplies

OPTIONAL
- prizes or treats

Kids get a kick out of following trail markers through the woods. This plan for an indoor hike gives your child a chance to follow the trail and to make new paths of his or her own. Best of all, he or she can be back in the kitchen for lunch or dinner.

You can mark the first trail for your hiker to follow by strategically placing socks as you weave along through rooms and hallways. Each sock should always be within sight of the previous one. Work with your child to create some simple rules, like having the toe of each sock always point to the next marker.

You can also add variety by turning the hike into a treasure hunt. Simply write clues on pieces of paper to put inside the socks that will direct your child to hidden treasures along the way: For example, "Proceed three more markers and find a small square object four paces from the trail."

After your explorer successfully follows your trail through the house, have him or her mark a route for you to follow. Now hit the trail, there's adventure ahead. . . .

CATEGORY
At Home

Trained Guesses

A train trip is a nice change from car travel for your family; there's always lots to see and plenty going on close at hand. Why not play this game to get your kids guessing about the trip and observing more at the same time?

To play, you ask your children questions relating to the trip, and they try to guess the answers. Then have everyone watch for the right answer. After a few questions and guesses, your kids will probably want to ask questions, too. Here are some sample questions:

REQUIRED
• writing supplies

- How long until the next station?

- How many cars will be waiting at the next crossing?

- How soon until another train passes going the other way?

- How many minutes before the conductor comes back into this car?

If you have older children, put them in charge of writing down the questions and guesses.

And look for opportunities to ask your children more questions about their guesses. Before you know it, they'll be experts at rail travel!

CATEGORY
On the Road

84

Travel Tally

REQUIRED
• writing supplies

If your children are entertained by counting things along the highway or rail tracks but are bored with the usual categories of trucks, buses, and license plates from home, try this twist for some variety.

To get your children started, give them some unusual categories of things they can count and have them keep a tally on a piece of paper. You might include silly categories, such as cars driven by men with mustaches, or elaborate ones, like trucks with red lettering going downhill.

You might also try having your children tally items by color, by size ("smaller than the car," "bigger than the car," or "bigger than a truck"), or by building type (restaurants, gas stations, office buildings, etc.).

Depending on the region you're passing through, you may want to limit the viewing area so your children can keep up with the tally. But remember, accuracy doesn't count nearly as much as fun!

CATEGORY
On the Road

Traveling Board Games

When the miles get monotonous, pull out the Card Game Board (see activity 46) you made before you left home, and pass the time with some new twists on old favorites.

Highway lotto. Fill the game board pockets with cards placed face up. Every time someone spots something outside the window that matches the image on one of the cards, remove that card. The object of the game is to remove all of the cards in a specified amount of time or by a specified distance.

Highway bingo. To start the game, place the cards in the pockets face up. Every time one of the objects is spotted, turn that card over. Players try to get a complete row or column in the shortest time possible, then call "bingo!" (or a term of your own choosing).

Highway concentration. Fill the pockets randomly with paired images, inserting them face down. Have your children take turns looking for pairs by turning over two cards at a time. When a pair is found, remove the two cards and give the finder a free turn.

While you've got the game board out, also try the games in activity 101 and then see if your kids can invent their own games. When you get back home, you might even be able to market them and pay for a few future vacations.

REQUIRED
- Make-Before-You-Go Card Game Board (see activity 46)

CATEGORY
On the Road

86

⚠ **adult supervision**

You (and Me) Tube Heads

REQUIRED
- large cardboard box
- art supplies
- yogurt container lids
- writing supplies

How would your child like to produce a video (using no camera or microphone) that's sure to go viral – at least, among your family members? Best of all, you don't even have to power on your computer or tablet to see the show.

To make some "tube head" gear, take a box at least 18 by 18 by 18 inches and cut out a "screen" in front, as well as a hole in the bottom large enough for a person's head to comfortably fit through. Have your child draw a button or two under the screen, or affix yogurt container lids; these are the "controls" for the "monitor."

Next, have your child write a video guide including the video's name and description. "Viewers" then take turns choosing the videos for your tube head child to "stream" (act out). For added fun, groups of kids can wear their own tube head gear and become part of the video.

Who says it's complicated to produce 3-D videos?

CATEGORY
At Home

Tunnel Vision

The changing world outside the window of a car or train provides a lot of things for your child to look at. This activity will enable him or her to get a different view of the scenery.

To play, all your child needs is a rolled-up piece of paper or a cardboard paper towel or toilet paper tube. Your child places the tube up to one eye, closes the other, and watches the passing scenery for a short amount of time (one minute is plenty). Then the child describes what he or she saw in as much detail as possible, based on the view through the tube. You might need to ask some questions to get the descriptions rolling, such as, "Did you see the red house?" You can also ask questions about things that weren't there—like a brown cow—and listen to the detailed descriptions of the phantom animal!

As a variation, have your child provide a running commentary as he or she watches the passing scenery through the tube. You can also vary the game by limiting how much the tube can be moved around. It will be a fun challenge for your child to describe unfamiliar territory from a decidedly narrow view.

REQUIRED
• cardboard tube or paper

CATEGORY
On the Road

88

⚠ small parts

REQUIRED
- coins
- spoons
- cups or bowls

Two-Bit Tiddlywinks

Tiddlywinks is an old favorite that involves snapping plastic disks into a target cup. Here's a do-it-yourself version that takes just small change to put together.

The idea of the game is to use a spoon to flip coins into a cup or bowl placed in the center of the table. Place the coins on the handle of a spoon, with the handle pointing away from the target. Gently tap the spoon so that the coin is launched into the air toward the target. After demonstrating how the launcher works, have the players experiment with different coins and different spoons to find the best combination.

For variety, add smaller and larger targets and assign a point value to each—the smaller the target, the higher the points.

One thing you can be sure of: Your children will flip when they get their two cents in!

CATEGORY
At Home

Upside Down

It's rumored (in our household, anyway), that when Leonardo da Vinci got stuck for artistic inspiration, he occasionally drew a picture upside down. In fact, that may just be why the Mona Lisa's smile looks so weird—she was da Vinci's first attempt at upside-down drawing!

See whether your child can improve upon such primitive artistic efforts by using today's modern drawing tools (paper, pencil, and eraser). Give your child a subject, and see whether your child can draw it from the bottom up. For example, if your child is drawing a person, he or she starts with the model's shoes, moves up to the legs, then the arms, then the torso, then the neck, head, and hair. You might establish other tricky drawing rules, too: Your child draws the right side of the subject and then the left side, or draws the details and then the outlines, and so on. You might be surprised at the results.

So why is the statue of the mayor wearing its hat on its feet? Now, hold on a minute. The paper is upside down!

REQUIRED
• drawing supplies

CATEGORY
Anytime, Anyplace

90 Vegetable Art

Here's a fun activity for your child to do while you're cutting fresh vegetables—you might call it "art you can eat!"

As you cut and chop, give your child the discarded vegetable pieces to assemble as a collage on a tray or plate. He or she might also draw the outline of a person's face, an animal, or an object, then use the vegetable pieces for features or details. Carrot ends, for instance, make wonderful eyes or wheels. For a vegetable landscape, your child can use small celery stalks to create a forest. The end of a cucumber will certainly make a fine nose or a mountain.

It helps if you cut the scraps into a variety of sizes and shapes, and you may also want to include a few pieces that aren't scraps—broccoli florets, for instance, can make great hair for a vegetable head.

Whatever the outcome, you and your child are sure to agree that his or her picture is indeed very tasteful art!

REQUIRED
• vegetable trimmings
• plate or tray

CATEGORY
In the Kitchen

Waitperson of the Hour

And today's chef's surprise is the noodles with snake toes and broccoli wings, gently broiled at four thousand degrees for six days and served on a lush bed of tree bark!

If your kids are in a silly mood while you're waiting for a meal at a restaurant, let them take turns putting their energy to good use inventing and describing fantasy specials. To make it a team effort, each person adds an ingredient or cooking technique.

OPTIONAL
• writing supplies
• menu

Alternatively, your junior waitpeople can look at the actual menu and offer descriptions (real or imaginary) of each item—the ingredients, how the dish is prepared, its unique nutritional benefits, why it's the house special, and so on.

If you have a pad and pencil with you, the junior waitperson can also take down the orders, noting any special requests for food preparations or substitutions.

And speaking of substitutions, sorry, but there aren't any for the tree bark—that's what makes the dish so rich in Vitamin Z48!

CATEGORY
Out and About

92

Wall Mural

REQUIRED
- large sheets of paper
- masking tape
- art supplies

Do you sometimes wish you had different views from the windows in your house? Why not have your kids create a mural that illustrates that real or imaginary view?

Begin by taping pieces of paper together to form a larger sheet to tape to the wall. Have your child draw a window frame or door frame at the edge of the paper and then draw or paint a whimsical scene beyond the opening— perhaps a barn with cows and chickens or a prehistoric jungle suddenly appears next door to your house through the brand new window, or perhaps a friend and her pet giraffe is arriving at the door!

Alternatively, your kids might draw the actual view that they see from your window or door frame. Perhaps they see your neighbor's house, a park, or even a lake. Ask your kids to look out a window or door and draw what they actually see. Or, for an extra challenge, see whether they can recreate the view from memory. Bet you never noticed the hippo lying on the next door neighbor's porch!

CATEGORY
At Home

What Character!

Here's a proven boredom buster designed for a child who enjoys dress-up games.

Gather some accessories (hats, gloves, jewelry, scarves, etc.), clothing (oversized shirts, socks, shoes, and the like), and a variety of props (a briefcase, a newspaper, sports equipment, and so on). Then have your child hop "onstage" (a space you designate for the performance). Now give your child an item or two. He or she can put on the "costume" (or hold it, if appropriate) and undergo a theatrical transformation.

Have your child introduce him- or herself, give basic facts (name, age, place of residence), and elaborate on his or her background. Your child might also sing a song or tell a story in character.

You can ask the character questions to reveal additional information. And be sure to find out why he or she is wearing your child's favorite sweatshirt . . . .

REQUIRED
• clothing, props and accessories

CATEGORY
At Home

94

What Did You Say!

Need a challenging game with a different slant? Then try this.

Assign someone the role of "it." That person tries to keep from speaking despite the efforts of everyone else to make him or her talk. Depending on the age of the players, this may be relatively easy—perhaps asking a young child a simple yes-or-no question. For older players, it might take some ingenuity: asking questions nonchalantly like, "Anyone see that thing that just flew in the window?"

REQUIRED
• your time only

If ingenuity doesn't have the desired effect, perhaps some tall tales will. Someone can simply take advantage of the opportunity to spin endless, pointless yarns without interruption. That's sure to make "it" crack!

Alternatively, make the object of the game to get someone to laugh by telling jokes, making funny faces, or asking silly questions. You and your family will probably find it almost impossible to refrain from laughing when the goal is to be serious.

CATEGORY
Anytime, Anyplace

What Would They Do?

We've all thought it: You're stuck in some kind of difficult situation and you wonder what your favorite person—a friend you admire, even a storybook hero—would do in similar circumstances. The same idea can turn any wait into a game. And when you play in the doctor's office, the game can give your child the encouragement he or she needs to get through an anxious situation.

Here's how to get started. Take quick stock of your surroundings. Are you waiting to see the dentist? Ask your children what they think their favorite storybook character might do if he or she were visiting the dentist. What kind of dentist would Goldilocks visit? And what would the dentist say to Goldilocks? "Somebody's been sitting in my chair and it fits just right!"

What about the doctor? What kind of doctor would Mrs. Tiggy-winkle visit? What would be her problem? "I just can't seem to lose any weight." "Well," the doctor might say, "have you tried making your dish run away with a spoon?"

REQUIRED
• your time only

CATEGORY
Out and About

96 Which Thing Came First?

Your children are surrounded by gadgets, widgets, and inventions that affect almost everything they do—some very new, and some surprisingly old. Do your kids know when ice cream and bicycles were invented? Test their historical knowledge with this quiz.

Read this starter list of items to your kids and have them tell you which came first—you can read two at a time, or more for older children. After your children put the list in order, see how close they can come to getting the actual year for each invention.

REQUIRED
• your time only

- modern bicycle—1880

- ice cream—2000 B.C.E.

- automobile—1908

- airplane—1903

- electronic computer—1946

- hot-air balloon—1783

- television—1939

- wheel—about 3000 B.C.E.

- coins—600 B.C.E.

CATEGORY
Anytime, Anyplace

- paper—105 A.D.

You and your child can take turns researching and writing lists. Fascinating—4,000 years of asking "One or two scoops!"

Who Knows What Fun Lurks . . .

The world of shadows is its own place, where familiar objects like people, houses, and cars take on strange shapes. You and your kids can make that world your own with this playful activity.

The easiest way to play is to have your kids look for shadows on the ground, then associate them with the objects that make the image. This game can get really interesting in the late afternoon hours, when images become elongated because of the low angle of the sun.

REQUIRED
• your time only

Alternatively, let kids make their own shadow theater on the sidewalk. Hands can become animals or machines. Kids can also line up behind one another and make a multi-armed shadow.

Try standing in different places so that the heads of your shadows touch. Move your arms and legs to make a human shadow kaleidoscope—a shadowscope?

You can play these games whenever you have a sunny day and a long walk. After all, you've got to make play while the sun shines!

CATEGORY
Out and About

98

⚠ adult supervision

Witches' Brew

Eye of newt, tongue of frog, turtle's breath, and moss from log. How come imaginary witches and magicians have all the fun? Your kids can concoct their own magic potions right in the kitchen.

Provide your kids with a variety of ingredients: spices, flour, cornstarch, pasta, ketchup, mustard, oil, cracker crumbs, stale bread, food coloring, vinegar, and baking soda (to add "fizz"). Also needed are bowls, spoons, a whisk, and measuring cups. Now turn your kids loose, and remember, the more disgusting their concoction, the better!

Encourage your children to be "scientific" about their magic by measuring carefully and adding the ingredients at just the "right" time. To get in the true witches' brew spirit, ask them to describe their ingredients (mustard might be extract of bird feather) and the kind of magic the potion will make. Will it turn the cat into a dinosaur, make someone invisible, or melt a hole in the ground for a swimming pool?

Stir a bowl of gruesome mix, this witches' brew will work some tricks. . . .

REQUIRED
- common cooking ingredients
- bowls
- measuring cups
- spoons
- kitchen utensils

CATEGORY
In the Kitchen

With Apologies to Mr. Webster

Festoon, flabbergast, floccinaucinihilipilification. Would your child recognize these as real words? (The last one means to trivialize something.)

Offer your kids a list of words that sound as if they could be made up—like "onomatopoeia" or "cacophonous." Present an equal number that are actually made up, but sound real, like "flontipulate" or "diathonkuling." See if your kids can spot the ringers from the bona fide dictionary entries. (You might want to browse through the dictionary or keep a "weird but true" list of words handy. Look for entries like "siderdromophobia," which, believe it or not, means a fear of train travel.) Or, you might want to use words from your profession.

As a variation, ask your kids to guess what the words mean. You're bound to learn some amazing facts—like how "floccinaucinihilipilification" has to do with the process of helping hippos take care of their teeth!

REQUIRED
• your time only

CATEGORY
Anytime, Anyplace

100 Word Family Game

This game may be tame, but it's not the same as one that's lame. Your kids won't shun this fun in the sun or on the run. In fact, they may stop whining, drop what they're doing, and hop to attention.

To play, have your kids try to make a sentence using four words from a "word family" (a group of words that share beginnings or endings). For example:

REQUIRED
• your time only

- The mole in the hole stole a pole.

- The cat spat at the rat.

- The big rigs haul twigs and figs.

- The thin pin is in the bin.

Other word families your kids can use are those that end with *-an, -at, -it, -et, -ug, -en, -og, -op, -un, -ame, -ind, -ine, and -ing*.

As your kids get good at making up these silly sentences, have them try for more than four words in each. And, of course, humor counts!

So, hug a bug and lug a rug; scan the plan to man the flan; this quiz has a quiet quality that will quadruple your quotient of quick entertainment.

CATEGORY
Anytime, Anyplace

Word Games Galore

101

Here are four word games you can do with the Card Game Board (see activity 46) you made before you left home.

Hidden words. Place the letters in pockets to make words horizontally, vertically, and diagonally, then cover the letters with the other game cards. Take turns uncovering and recovering a single letter. When someone thinks he or she knows the location of an entire word, that person can uncover all of the letters in that word.

Rows and Columns. Randomly place letters on the board and take turns forming as many words as possible with the letters in a single row or column. Set a time limit or use the car's odometer.

Quick spell. Place all of the letters facedown on the board, then pick one at random for each child's turn. That player then has to find an object that begins with that letter and spell it.

Don't hesitate to make up your own word games, too. No one will get bored with this board!

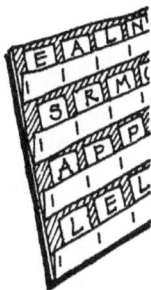

REQUIRED
• Make-Before-You-Go Card Game Board (see activity 46)

CATEGORY
On the Road

ABOUT THE AUTHORS

Steve and Ruth Bennett are the authors of the million copy-selling activity books, *365 TV-Free Activities You Can Do With Your Child* and *365 Outdoor Activities You Can Do With Your Child*, as well as numerous other activity books. The Bennetts have written widely on families and quality time. Steve is an expert on digital technologies; Ruth is a landscape architect who specializes in public parks, university quadrangles, and children's play spaces. They have two young-adult children and live in Cambridge, MA.

INDEX

Get 'em Moving

In the Kitchen

Imagine This

On the Road

Word Games

Younger Kids Play

Your Time Only

We Welcome Your Feedback!

Do you have any great offline activities that are favorites in your family? If you'd like to share them with us, please email us at:

ideas@offlineactivities.com

If we use your idea(s) in future editions, we'll be sure to give you credit in the book. (All entries become the sole property of Steve and Ruth Bennett.)